A Kalmus Classic Edition

Leopold

MOZART

TWELVE DUETS

For Two Violins

K 04608

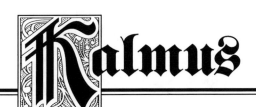
Kalmus

12
Duette

Leopold Mozart

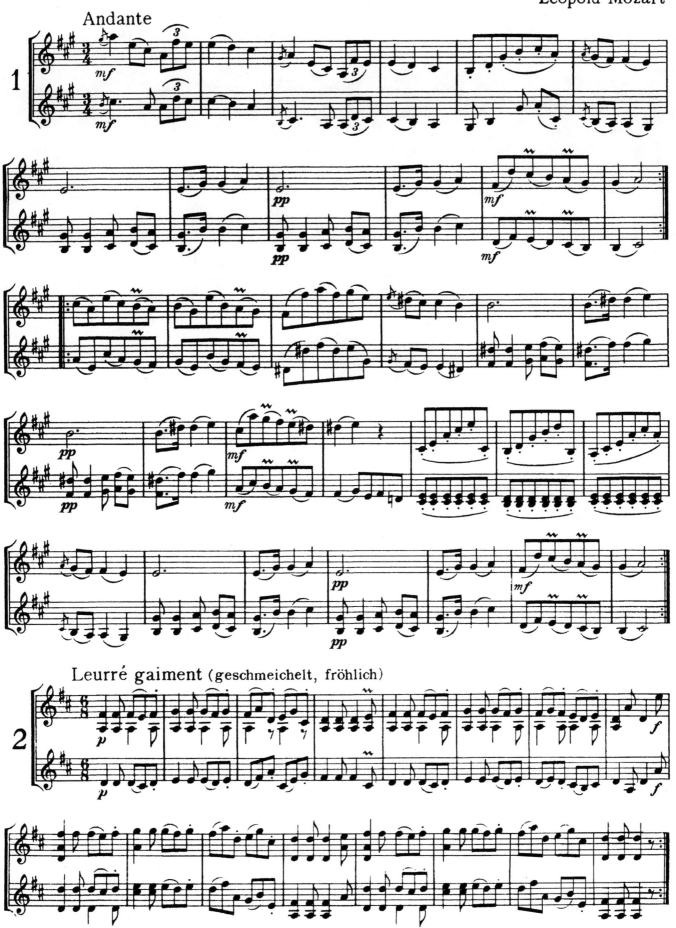

4

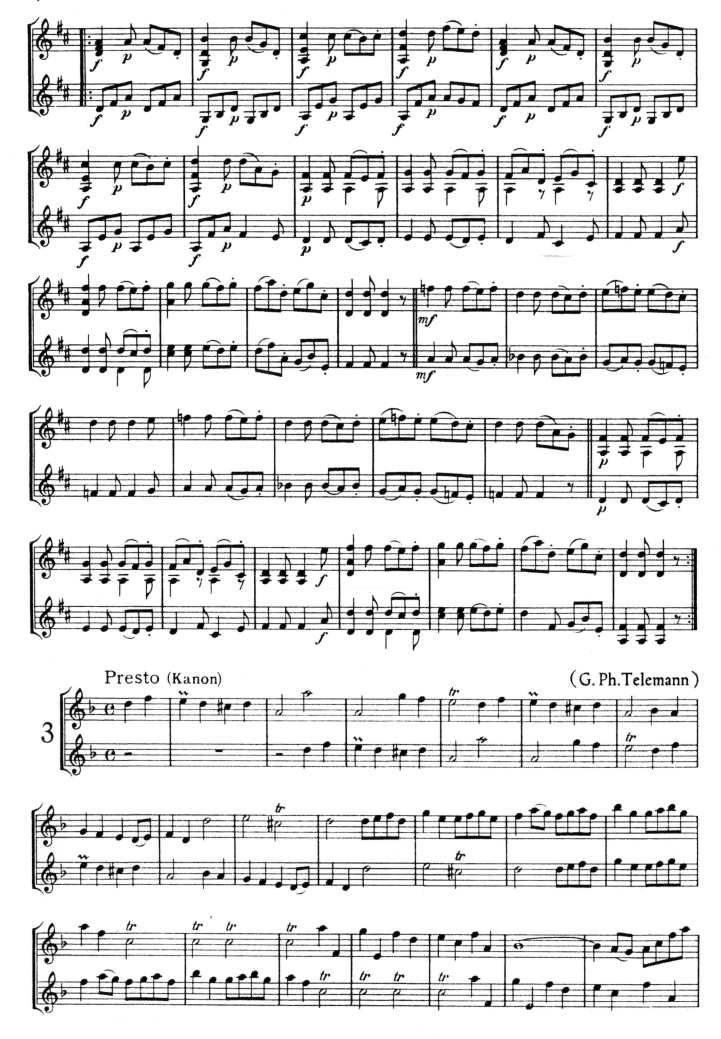

Presto (Kanon)

(G. Ph. Telemann)

3

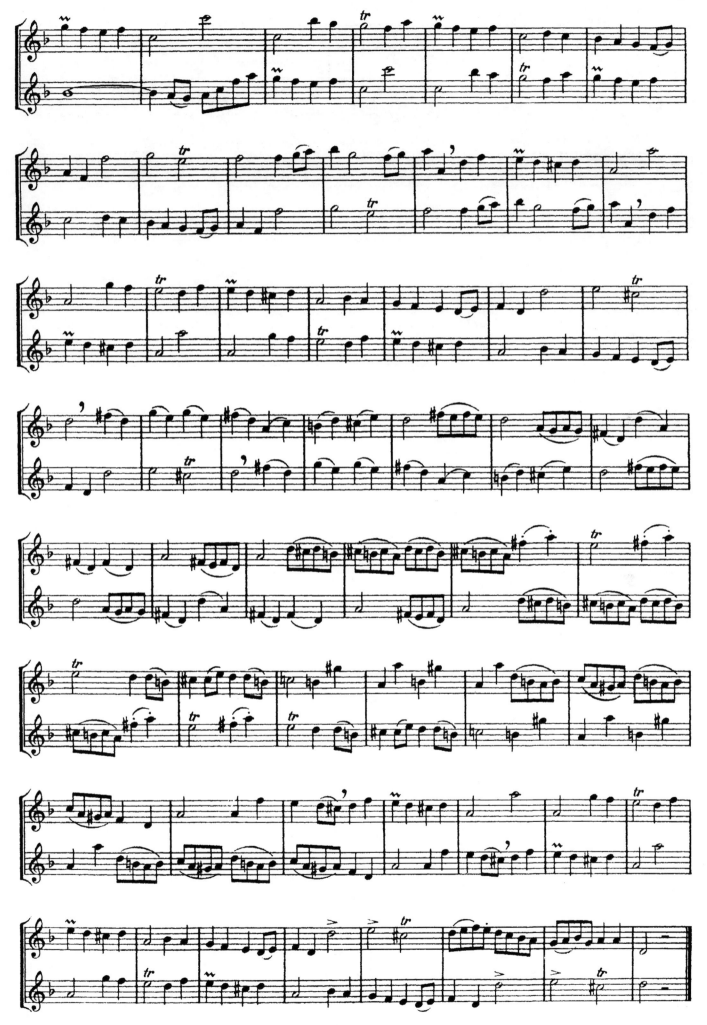

6

Tempo di minuetto

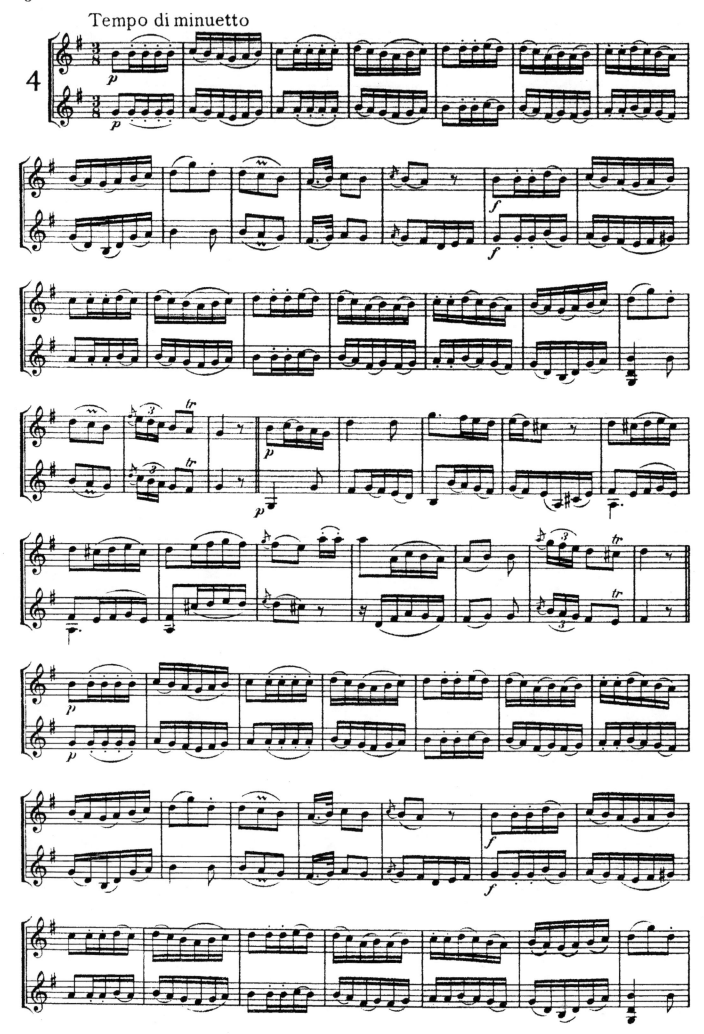

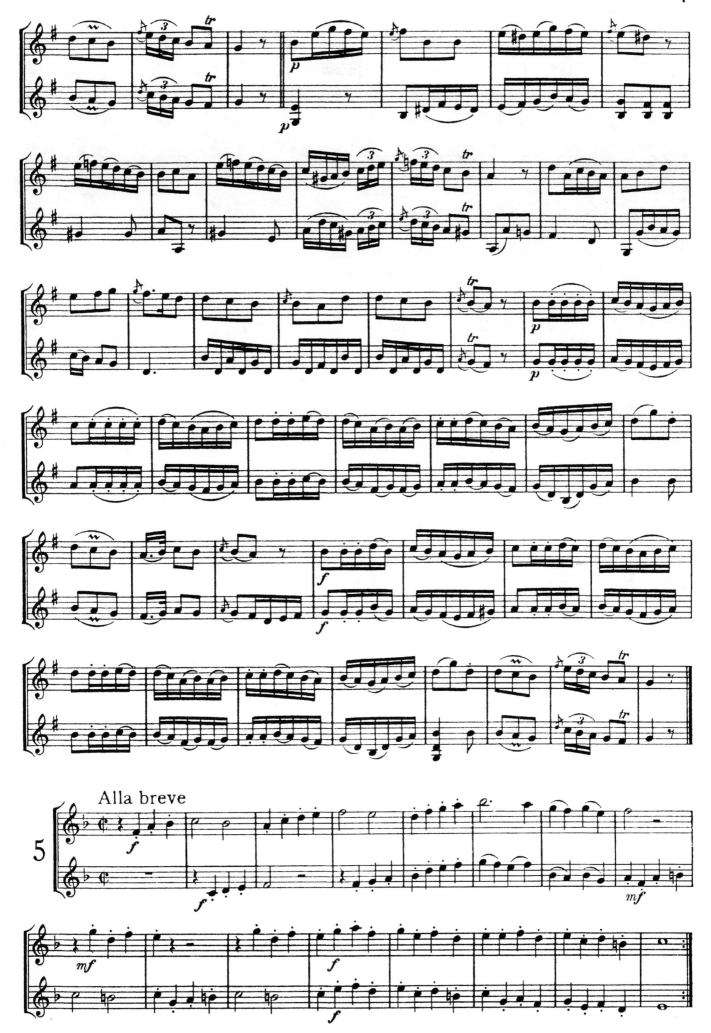

8

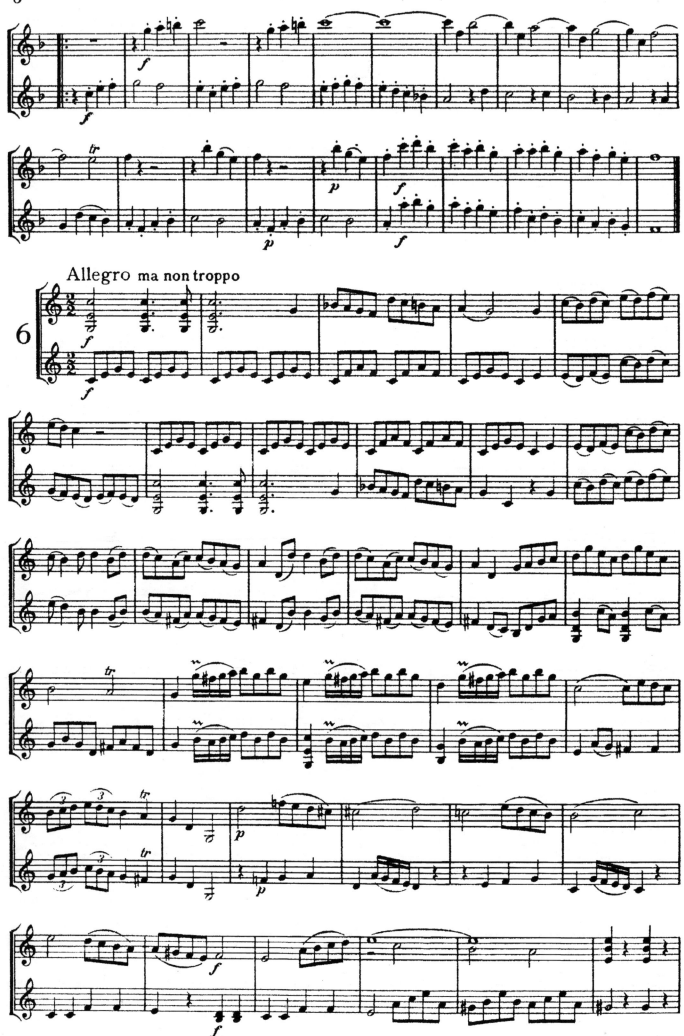

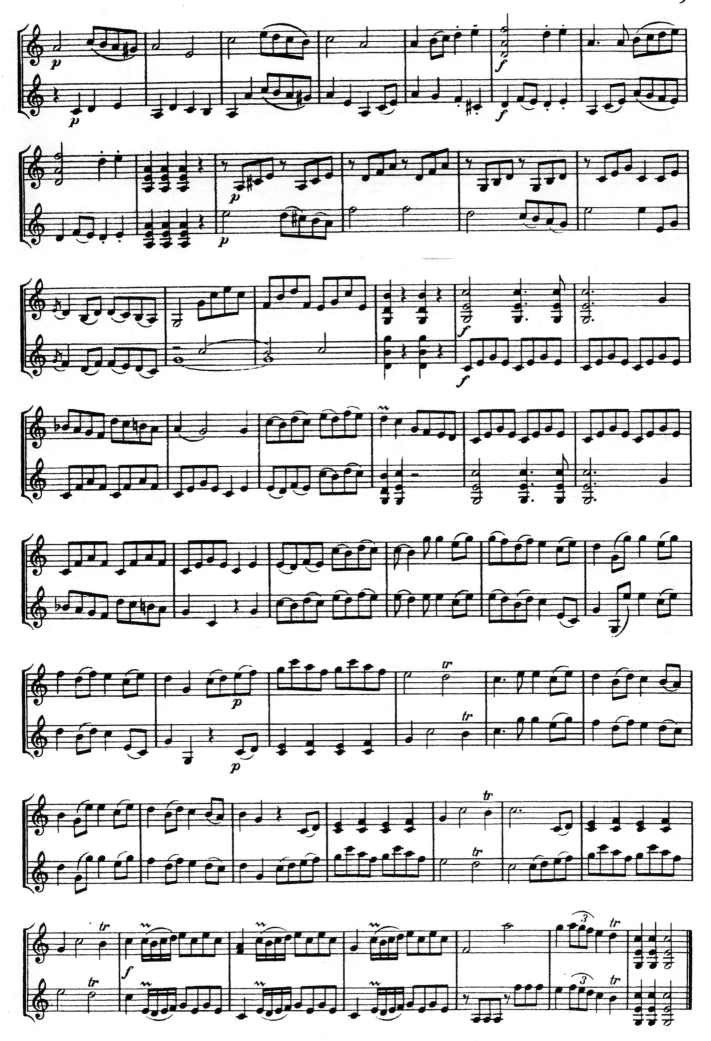

(G. Ph. Telemann)

Presto (Kanon)

7

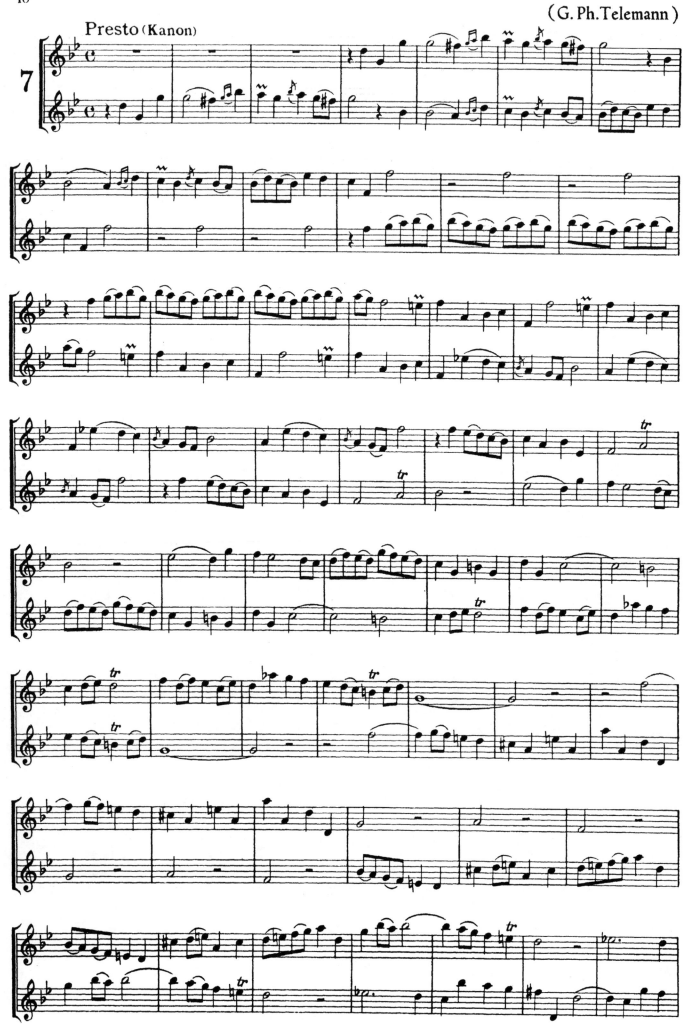

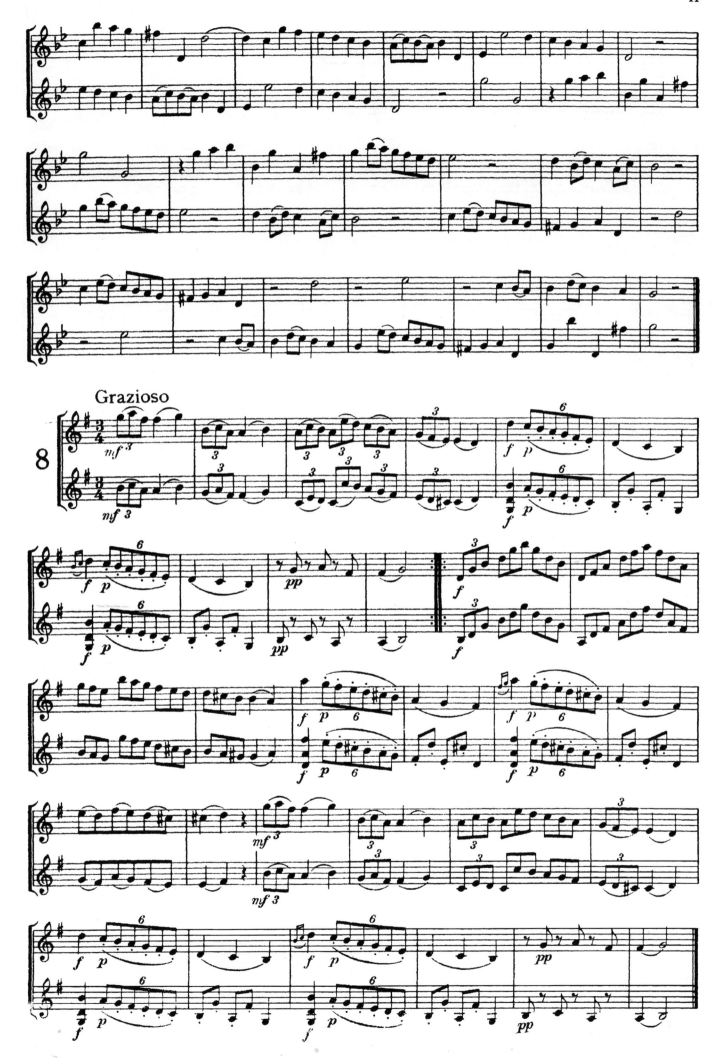

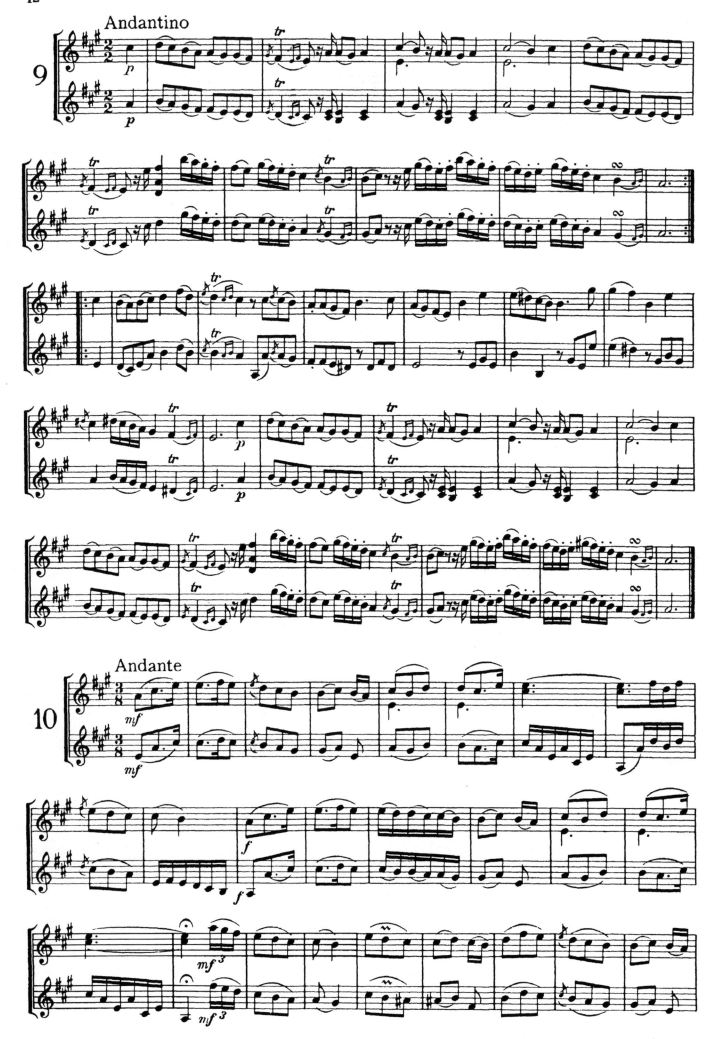

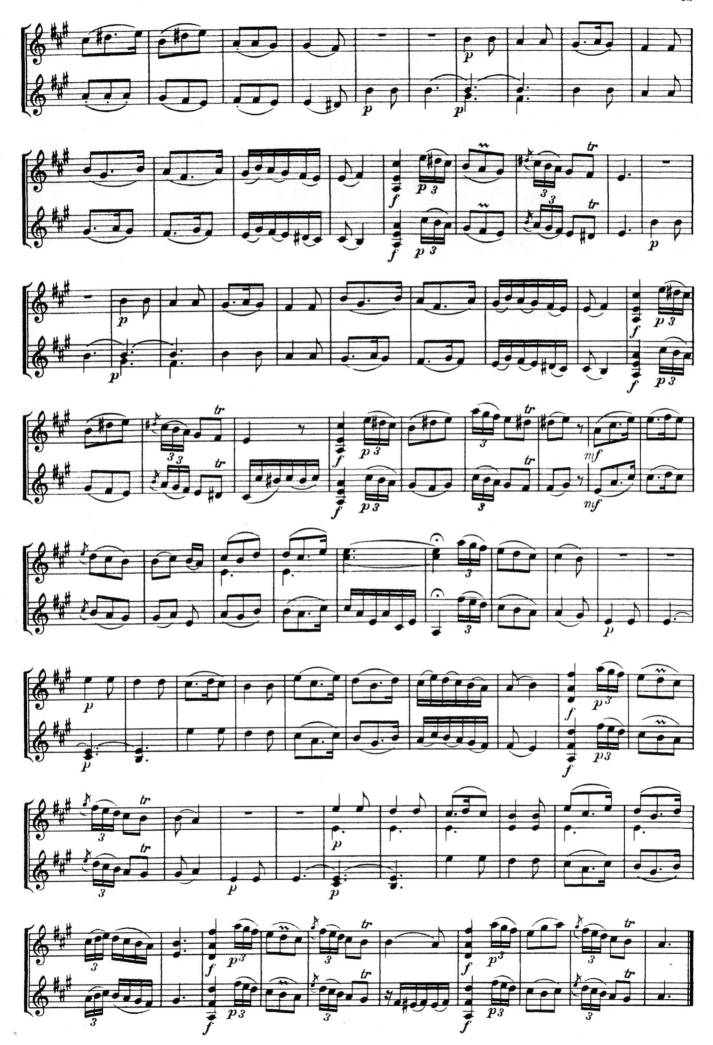

14

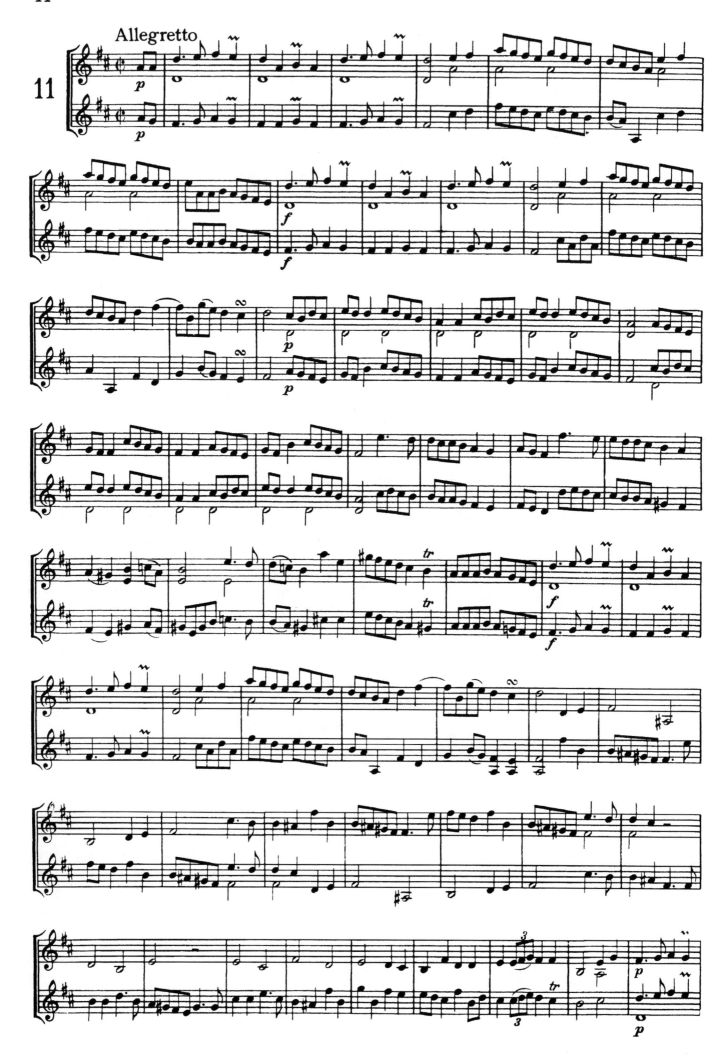

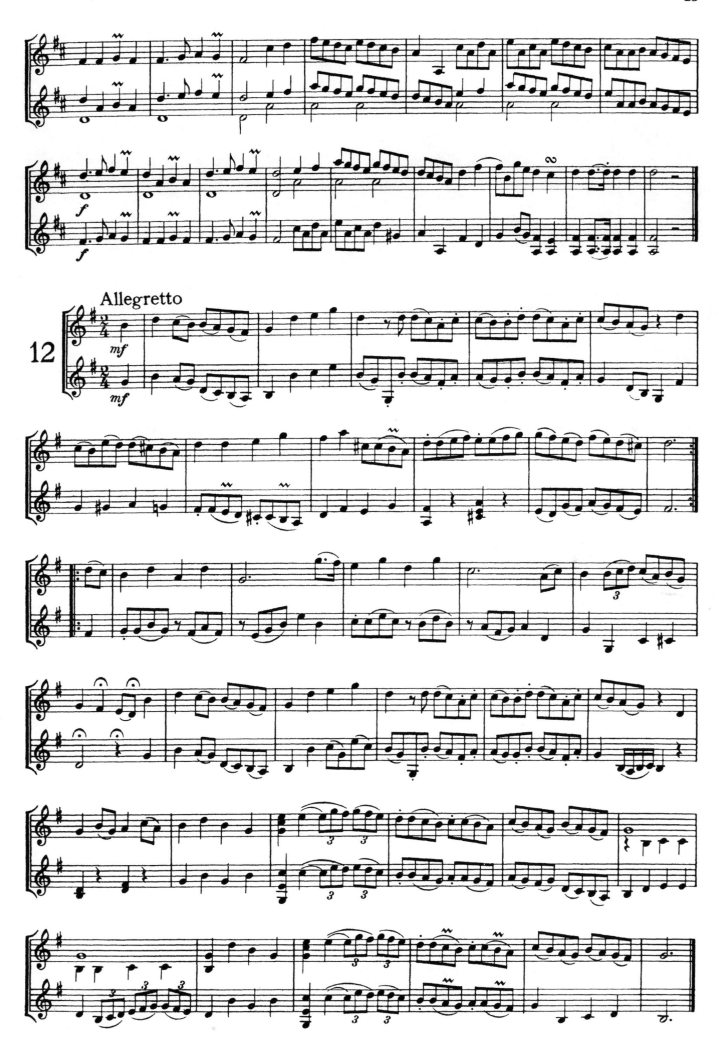

Allegretto

12

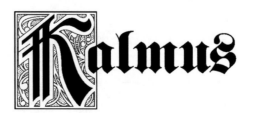